# WATCHING THE WATCHERS

## The U.S. Constitution, Police Power, and What Every Cop Watcher Must Know

**Written by:**
**Special Ed**

# Introduction — Watching the Watchers

In the United States, police power does not exist in a vacuum. It exists only because the people allow it to exist—and only within strict constitutional limits. Cop watching is not a provocation, a loophole, or a fringe activity. It is a **lawful, constitutionally grounded act of civic oversight**, rooted in the same principles that gave rise to the American republic.

The U.S. Constitution was written with a deep mistrust of unchecked authority. Its authors had lived under arbitrary enforcement, secret policing, and retaliation against dissent. As a result, they built a system where **government actors are accountable to the public**, not shielded from it. Police officers, as agents of the state, are not exempt from this design. When they act in public, exercising public authority, they do so under the gaze of the people.

Cop watching exists because accountability requires observation. Abuse flourishes in darkness; liberty survives in the open.

This book is written for **ordinary people**—not lawyers, not judges, not credentialed journalists—who want to understand what the Constitution actually says about observing, recording, and questioning police conduct. You do not need permission to know your rights. You do not need a press badge to invoke them. And you do not surrender them because an officer feels uncomfortable, annoyed, or challenged.

Over the past several decades, technology has placed powerful tools in the hands of citizens. A phone camera can document truth faster than an internal investigation. Video evidence has exonerated the innocent, exposed misconduct, and forced accountability where silence once prevailed. In response, some law enforcement agencies have embraced transparency. Others have resisted it—sometimes aggressively.

This resistance is not new. Historically, whenever citizens have asserted their rights—whether to speak, to publish, to assemble, or to observe—the state has often responded by testing the limits of those rights. Cop watchers sit directly at that fault line. Knowing the Constitution is what keeps that line from being crossed.

This book exists for one purpose: **to translate constitutional law into practical knowledge for cop watchers**. It explains:

- Which amendments protect your right to observe and record police
- What police can lawfully demand—and what they cannot
- How the First, Fourth, Fifth, and other amendments work together
- Why filming police is not interference
- How courts have repeatedly affirmed these rights
- How to protect yourself during real-world encounters

This is not a call to confrontation. It is a call to **informed presence**. A knowledgeable cop watcher is calm, lawful, and grounded in constitutional reality. Rights are strongest when exercised responsibly—and weakest when misunderstood or abandoned out of fear.

Police officers are not your enemies by default. But neither are they above scrutiny. The Constitution does not ask citizens to trust blindly. It asks them to **remain vigilant**.

Cop watching is the modern expression of an old idea:

*In a free society, those who wield power must be seen.*

This book is your guide to seeing clearly—and lawfully.

# Chapter 1 — The Constitution Was Written to Watch Power

The United States Constitution was not written to make government efficient. It was written to make government **limited**.

Every right discussed in this book—speech, silence, privacy, due process—exists because the people who drafted the Constitution understood a dangerous truth: **power, when unobserved, will eventually abuse itself**. Cop watching is not a modern invention. It is the natural continuation of the Constitution's core purpose—public oversight of state authority.

## Government Power Is Conditional

Police authority is **delegated power**, not inherent power. Officers do not possess authority because of personal status, uniform, or intent. They possess authority only because the Constitution permits it—and only within constitutional boundaries.

When police stop a person, detain them, search them, question them, or use force, they are exercising the most intrusive powers the state possesses. In a free society, those powers must be:

- Visible
- Justifiable
- Reviewable
- Challengeable

Cop watching exists because secrecy and liberty cannot coexist.

## Public Space Means Public Accountability

A foundational principle of constitutional law is simple:

> **What the government does in public may be observed by the public.**

Police officers performing official duties in public places—streets, sidewalks, parks, plazas—have **no reasonable expectation of privacy** in those actions. This is not disrespectful. It is structural. The law recognizes that transparency is a safeguard against abuse.

Recording police activity is not surveillance of private individuals. It is documentation of **state conduct**.

## The Constitution Does Not Require Permission

One of the most common misunderstandings—encouraged by intimidation and misinformation—is the idea that citizens must obtain permission to observe police. This is false.

The Constitution does not say:

- "You may speak if approved"
- "You may record if authorized"
- "You may observe if officers consent"

Rights do not come from compliance. They come from **citizenship**.

If your conduct is lawful, silent, non-obstructive, and in a public place, you are not required to justify it to anyone.

## Cop Watching Is Not Interference

Police often frame observation as "interference" when what they really mean is **discomfort**. The Constitution does not protect officers from discomfort. It protects citizens from abuse of authority.

Interference requires **actual obstruction**, not:

- Filming
- Standing nearby
- Narrating events
- Asking lawful questions
- Criticizing police conduct

Observation becomes interference only when it physically prevents officers from performing a lawful duty. Courts have consistently rejected the idea that scrutiny itself is obstruction.

## Why Police Sometimes Push Back

Police resistance to cop watching is rarely about safety. It is usually about:

- Control
- Authority
- Narrative dominance
- Avoidance of accountability

When police discourage filming, demand explanations, or threaten arrest without legal basis, they are often **testing your knowledge**, not enforcing the law.

The Constitution anticipates this. That is why it:

- Separates powers
- Limits discretion
- Requires justification
- Protects silence

Cop watching is not anti-police. It is **pro-Constitution**.

## Rights Are Strongest When Exercised Calmly

The Constitution does not reward chaos. A cop watcher who understands their rights:

- Remains calm
- Uses clear language
- Knows when to speak and when to stay silent
- Understands when a command is lawful—and when it is not

You do not need to win an argument on the street. You need to **protect your rights** and preserve evidence. The courtroom—not the sidewalk—is where unlawful conduct is resolved.

## The Amendments Work Together

Cop watching is not protected by a single sentence or clause. It is protected by a **constitutional framework**, including:

- The First Amendment (speech, press, accountability)
- The Fourth Amendment (freedom from unreasonable seizure)
- The Fifth Amendment (silence and self-protection)
- The Fourteenth Amendment (equal protection and due process)
- The Ninth Amendment (retained rights of the people)

This book will break down each of these protections clearly, practically, and without legal jargon.

## The Central Truth of Cop Watching

Cop watching exists because **freedom requires witnesses**.

The Constitution does not ask citizens to trust power blindly. It asks them to **observe it**, question it, and hold it accountable—peacefully, lawfully, and persistently.

That is not radical.

That is American.

# Chapter 2 — The First Amendment: Speech, Press, and the Right to Record Police

The First Amendment is the **core constitutional protection for cop watchers.** It is the amendment that turns observation into a right instead of a favor, and documentation into protected conduct rather than suspicious behavior.

At its heart, the First Amendment exists to prevent government officials from controlling information about their own actions. Police officers are government officials. When they act in public, they do so under the authority of the state—and the First Amendment ensures the public may see, hear, and record what that authority looks like in practice.

## What the First Amendment Actually Protects

The First Amendment protects five related freedoms:

- Speech
- Press
- Assembly
- Petition
- Religion

For cop watchers, **speech and press are the most critical.**

Importantly, the amendment does **not** define these freedoms narrowly. It does not say "professional press." It does not say "approved speech." It does not say "non-critical observation."

It protects **the act of gathering information** so that speech and publication can occur.

Courts have repeatedly recognized that:

> You cannot have freedom of speech or press without the freedom to gather information.

Recording police is information gathering.

## You Are the Press (Whether You Like It or Not)

One of the most persistent myths used against cop watchers is the idea that only journalists are protected by the press clause.

This is false.

The Constitution protects **activities**, not job titles.

If you are:

- Filming
- Photographing
- Livestreaming
- Taking notes
- Documenting events

You are engaging in press activity—even if you never publish the footage, even if you are filming only for personal records, and even if you strongly criticize police conduct.

The First Amendment does not require:

- Credentials
- Affiliation
- Neutrality
- Approval

A citizen with a phone has the same constitutional right to record police as a newsroom with a broadcast camera.

## Recording Police Is Protected Speech

Recording police is not merely passive observation. It is expressive conduct.

When you record:

- You create a record of government behavior
- You preserve evidence
- You enable later speech, criticism, or publication

Courts recognize that **preventing recording is functionally the same as suppressing speech**, because it stops the creation of information before it can be shared.

This is why officers may not lawfully order you to stop recording simply because:

- They dislike being filmed
- They claim it is "policy"
- They feel disrespected
- They say "you can't record me"

Policy does not override the Constitution.

## Criticism of Police Is Explicitly Protected

The First Amendment exists *because* government officials dislike criticism.

You may lawfully:

- Criticize police verbally
- Narrate their actions
- Ask questions
- Express disagreement
- Use harsh or offensive language

So long as your conduct does not rise to actual obstruction or a true threat, **offensive speech is still protected speech.**

Courts have repeatedly ruled that:

> Police officers are expected to endure more criticism than private citizens.

Discomfort is not a legal standard.

## Time, Place, and Manner Limits (What Police Can Actually Regulate)

The First Amendment is not unlimited, but its limits are narrow.

Police may impose **reasonable time, place, and manner restrictions**, but only if all three of the following are true:

1. The restriction is **content-neutral**
    - It applies regardless of whether speech is favorable or critical
2. It is **narrowly tailored**
    - It addresses a real safety or operational concern
3. It leaves **ample alternative channels** for recording

Orders that fail these tests—such as blanket bans on filming or arbitrary distance demands—are unconstitutional.

An officer cannot invent a restriction simply because filming makes them uncomfortable.

## Recording Is Not Interference

Police often misuse the word "interference" to suppress lawful observation.

Under First Amendment doctrine:

- Interference requires **actual obstruction**
- Recording alone is not obstruction
- Presence alone is not obstruction

Standing at a reasonable distance and filming silently is protected conduct.

Even verbal criticism does not become interference unless it **materially disrupts** police activity.

Annoyance is not obstruction. Scrutiny is not interference.

## Retaliation Violates the First Amendment

Police may not lawfully retaliate against protected speech.

Retaliation includes:

- Detaining you for filming
- Arresting you without legal cause
- Threatening arrest to stop recording
- Seizing equipment because of criticism

If police action is motivated by your protected speech rather than legitimate law enforcement objectives, it violates the First Amendment—even if the officer later claims a pretext.

## Why the First Amendment Matters Most at the Street Level

The First Amendment is strongest where it is most often tested: **on the sidewalk, during real encounters, under pressure.**

Police may lie.

Police may bluff.

Police may misstate the law.

The Constitution does not require you to debate them on the spot. It requires only that **your conduct remain lawful**.

Cop watching is protected not because it is convenient—but because it is necessary.

## The Core Rule for Cop Watchers

If you remember only one principle from this chapter, remember this:

> **You have a First Amendment right to record police performing their duties in public, so long as you do not physically interfere.**

Everything else—commands, threats, policies, irritation—comes second to that rule.

# Chapter 3 — The Fourth Amendment: Detention, ID Demands, and Unlawful Seizures

For cop watchers, the Fourth Amendment is the **line that police are not allowed to cross simply because they are being observed**. While the First Amendment protects your right to record, the Fourth Amendment protects your **body, movement, property, and devices** from unjustified police control.

Many conflicts between police and cop watchers do not begin with filming—they begin when officers attempt to **stop, detain, identify, or seize** someone who has done nothing unlawful. Understanding the Fourth Amendment is what prevents a lawful act of observation from turning into an unlawful detention.

## What the Fourth Amendment Actually Protects

The Fourth Amendment protects people from:

- Unreasonable searches
- Unreasonable seizures
- Arbitrary detention
- Government intrusion without justification

A **seizure** occurs when:

- You are not free to leave, **or**
- An officer orders you to stay, **or**

- Your movement is physically blocked, **or**
- Your property (including your phone) is taken

Police authority does not activate automatically. It must be **legally justified** at every step.

## Filming Police Is NOT Reasonable Suspicion

This point cannot be overstated:

> **Recording police, by itself, is not reasonable suspicion of a crime.**

Reasonable suspicion requires:

- Specific facts
- Articulable reasoning
- A connection to an actual crime

Filming does not meet this standard.
Watching does not meet this standard.
Criticizing police does not meet this standard.
If officers cannot point to a specific crime you are suspected of committing, **they cannot lawfully detain you**.

## Consensual Encounter vs. Detention

Police encounters fall into two categories:

### 1. Consensual Encounters

- Officers may speak to you

- You may ignore them
- You may walk away
- You do not have to answer questions

If you are free to leave, **you are not detained.**

**2. Detentions (Investigatory Stops)**

- You are ordered to stay
- You are not free to leave
- Police must have reasonable suspicion

Cop watchers are often treated as detained **without lawful justification.** This is a Fourth Amendment violation.

A simple and powerful question is:

**"Am I being detained, or am I free to go?"**

If you are free to go, you may leave.
If you are detained, the officer must justify it.

## ID Demands and the Fourth Amendment

Police often demand identification from cop watchers as a way to assert control. This demand is not automatically lawful.

Police may demand ID **only if:**

1. You are lawfully detained, **and**
2. State law explicitly requires ID during a lawful detention

If you are not detained, you generally have **no obligation** to identify yourself.

If an officer cannot articulate reasonable suspicion of a crime, **an ID demand is unlawful**.

Filming police does not trigger ID requirements.

## Detention Cannot Be Used as Punishment

Police may not use detention to:

- Discourage filming
- Identify critics
- "Check you out"
- Fish for violations

Detention must be:

- Temporary
- Purpose-driven
- Closely related to the suspected offense

Using detention as retaliation or intimidation violates both the Fourth and First Amendments.

## Searches of Cop Watchers

Police may not:

- Search your phone without a warrant
- Scroll through your videos
- Demand to see footage
- Force you to unlock your device

A phone is not just a camera—it is a container of private data. Courts recognize this distinction clearly.

Even during an arrest, police generally require a **warrant** to search the digital contents of a phone.

## Seizure of Cameras and Phones

Police may seize recording devices **only under narrow conditions**, such as:

- A valid warrant, or
- True exigent circumstances involving imminent destruction of evidence

Filming police does **not** create exigent circumstances.
Police may not:

- Delete footage
- Order deletion
- Destroy devices
- Threaten seizure to stop recording

Such actions are serious constitutional violations.

## The "Officer Safety" Excuse

"Officer safety" is often invoked—but it is not a blank check.

Safety concerns must be:

- Specific
- Articulable
- Reasonable

A generalized claim that filming makes an officer "nervous" is **not** sufficient to justify detention, search, or seizure.

Courts require more than discomfort.

## Distance Orders and the Fourth Amendment

Police may order distance **only if**:

- The order is lawful
- The order is related to safety or operations
- The distance is reasonable and specific

Arbitrary or excessive distance orders designed to prevent recording are unlawful.

If you comply with a lawful distance order and continue recording, **your rights remain intact**.

## Key Fourth Amendment Principles for Cop Watchers

- Observation is not suspicion
- Filming is not probable cause
- Discomfort is not a crime
- Retaliation is not enforcement
- Phones are protected property
- Silence is lawful
- Walking away is lawful (if not detained)

## The Fourth Amendment's Role in Cop Watching

The Fourth Amendment is what prevents police from converting **criticism into custody**.

It ensures that:

- Rights do not vanish under pressure
- Authority remains justified
- Power remains accountable

Cop watching would be meaningless if police could simply detain anyone who observes them. The Fourth Amendment exists to ensure that **watching power does not become a crime**.

# Chapter 4 — The Fifth Amendment: Silence, Questioning, and Self-Protection

If the First Amendment protects your **right to observe**, and the Fourth Amendment protects your **right to be left alone**, the Fifth Amendment protects your **right not to help the government build a case against you**.

For cop watchers, the Fifth Amendment is often the most misunderstood—and the most powerful—protection you have.

You do not need to explain yourself.

You do not need to justify your actions.

You do not need to answer questions to prove innocence.

The Constitution places the burden on the government—not on you.

## What the Fifth Amendment Actually Protects

The Fifth Amendment guarantees, among other things:

- The right against self-incrimination
- The right to remain silent
- Due process of law

The most important phrase for cop watchers is this:

> **No person "shall be compelled in any criminal case to be a witness against himself."**

This protection applies **before**, **during**, and **after** arrest.

## You Do Not Have to Answer Questions

Police questioning is not casual conversation. It is a **tool designed to extract information**—often to justify detention, escalation, or arrest after the fact.

You are not required to:

- Explain why you are filming
- Answer "what are you doing?"
- Explain where you are going
- State your intentions
- Engage in conversation

Silence is not obstruction.
Silence is not suspicious.
Silence is not a crime.

## The Right to Remain Silent Exists Before Arrest

A common myth is that the Fifth Amendment only applies after arrest or after Miranda warnings are given.

This is false.

Your right to remain silent exists:

- During consensual encounters
- During detentions
- During arrests

Miranda warnings protect statements made **after custodial interrogation**, but the **right itself exists at all times**.

You may invoke it at any moment.

## How to Invoke the Fifth Amendment

Silence alone may not always be enough. Courts often require that the right be **clearly asserted**.

Simple, lawful phrases include:

- "I am exercising my right to remain silent."
- "I do not answer questions."
- "I choose to remain silent."

Once you invoke your right:

- Police must stop questioning you
- Continued interrogation may violate the Constitution

You do not need to be polite.
You do not need to be hostile.
You need to be **clear**.

## Silence Cannot Be Used Against You

The Fifth Amendment prohibits:

- Using your silence as evidence of guilt
- Punishing you for refusing to answer
- Inferring criminal intent from silence

Police may attempt to pressure you by saying things like:

- "If you've got nothing to hide..."
- "Just answer a few questions..."

- "This will go easier if you cooperate..."

These statements have **no legal force**.
Cooperation is voluntary. Silence is constitutional.

## You Do Not Have to Explain Your Rights

Cop watchers are often baited into arguments about legality.
You do not need to:

- Explain the First Amendment
- Justify your presence
- Debate constitutional law

You are not required to educate police on the street.

Every word you speak is a potential tool against you. The Fifth Amendment exists to stop that process.

## Refusing Consent Is Not Incriminating

Police may ask for consent to:

- Search your phone
- View your footage
- Look through your belongings

You may lawfully say:

"I do not consent to any searches."

Refusing consent:

- Is not suspicious

- Does not justify detention
- Does not create probable cause

Consent is how constitutional protections are often bypassed. The Fifth Amendment protects you from being pressured into giving it.

## Silence During Detention

If you are lawfully detained, police may:

- Ask questions
- Attempt to identify you

But unless state law requires ID during lawful detention, you may still **remain silent.**

Answering questions during detention is **optional**, not mandatory.

## If You Are Arrested

If you are arrested:

1. Stop speaking immediately
2. Clearly invoke your right to remain silent
3. Ask for a lawyer

Once you request a lawyer:

- Police must stop questioning you
- Any continued interrogation may violate the Constitution

Never try to "talk your way out" of an arrest. That conversation will not help you.

## Why the Fifth Amendment Is Critical for Cop Watchers

Cop watchers are often targeted **not because they committed a crime**, but because police want to:

- Identify critics
- Create a pretext
- Intimidate observers
- Control the situation

The Fifth Amendment stops police from turning **lawful observation into self-incrimination**.

It protects you from:

- Saying something misunderstood
- Being misquoted
- Providing justification for unlawful action
- Escalation through words

Silence preserves evidence.
Silence preserves rights.
Silence preserves options.

## The Core Rule for Cop Watchers

Remember this:

**You cannot talk yourself into more rights—but you can talk yourself out of them.**

The Fifth Amendment is not about guilt.

It is about **power imbalance**.

Cop watching works best when paired with restraint, calm presence, and constitutional discipline.

# Chapter 5 — Other Constitutional Amendments That Protect Cop Watchers

Cop watching is most visibly protected by the First, Fourth, and Fifth Amendments—but it does not stand on those alone. Several **other constitutional amendments quietly reinforce your rights**, especially when police attempt to escalate encounters, apply laws selectively, or punish observation indirectly.

These amendments matter because **police encounters rarely stay confined to one constitutional issue.** When observation turns into detention, questioning, arrest, or prosecution, additional safeguards activate.

## The Sixth Amendment — Counsel, Confrontation, and Fair Process

The Sixth Amendment guarantees:

- The right to an attorney
- The right to a fair and speedy trial
- The right to confront witnesses
- The right to know the charges

For cop watchers, the Sixth Amendment becomes critical **after arrest or formal charges**, but its influence begins earlier.

### Why This Matters to Cop Watchers

Police sometimes arrest cop watchers not to secure a conviction, but to:

- Remove them from the scene
- Punish observation
- Create inconvenience or fear
- Assert authority

The Sixth Amendment ensures that:

- You are not left to navigate the system alone
- Police narratives are challengeable
- Evidence (including video) can be contested
- Retaliatory arrests do not escape scrutiny

If arrested, the correct response is simple:

**Invoke your right to remain silent and ask for a lawyer.**

From that moment forward, the Sixth Amendment shields you from being pressured into statements that support an unlawful arrest.

## The Fourteenth Amendment — Due Process and Equal Protection

The Fourteenth Amendment is one of the **most powerful protections for cop watchers**, especially at the state and local level.

It guarantees:

- Due process of law
- Equal protection under the law

It also applies the Bill of Rights to the states, meaning local and state police **must follow the same constitutional standards** as federal authorities.

### Due Process: No Arbitrary Enforcement

Due process means:

- Laws must be applied fairly
- Enforcement must be predictable
- Punishment cannot be arbitrary

Police may not:

- Invent charges to justify retaliation
- Apply vague laws selectively
- Enforce rules only against critics

If filming police leads to arrest while identical behavior by others is ignored, **due process is violated.**

### Equal Protection: No Targeting Cop Watchers

Equal protection prohibits selective enforcement based on:

- Viewpoint

- Criticism of police
- Association with oversight activity

If police tolerate:

- Tourists filming
- News crews recording
- Bystanders watching

—but target cop watchers for the same conduct, that disparity is constitutionally significant.

The Constitution does not allow police to punish **who you are or what you stand for**.

## The Ninth Amendment — Rights Retained by the People

The Ninth Amendment states that the listing of certain rights in the Constitution:

> "shall not be construed to deny or disparage others retained by the people."

This amendment is crucial because **no constitution can list every human right explicitly**.

Courts have relied on this principle to recognize:

- The right to gather information
- The right to observe government conduct
- The right to document public officials

Cop watching exists comfortably within this tradition.

Even where a right is not spelled out word-for-word, it may still be constitutionally protected if it aligns with liberty, accountability, and democratic oversight.

## The Tenth Amendment — Limits on Police Authority

The Tenth Amendment reminds us that:

- Powers not delegated to the federal government are reserved to the states or the people

Importantly, **police do not possess unlimited authority simply because they are local officials.**

Their power must:

- Come from valid law
- Align with constitutional limits
- Respect individual rights

Local ordinances, department policies, and officer preferences **do not override constitutional protections.**

## How These Amendments Work Together

Cop watching is protected not by a single clause, but by **constitutional layering**:

- The First Amendment protects observation and recording
- The Fourth Amendment prevents unjustified detention

- The Fifth Amendment protects silence and consent
- The Sixth Amendment protects you after arrest
- The Fourteenth Amendment ensures fairness and equality
- The Ninth Amendment preserves unlisted rights
- The Tenth Amendment limits police power

This overlap is intentional. The Constitution assumes power will push boundaries—and it responds by reinforcing rights from multiple angles.

## Why Police Often Ignore These Amendments

Street-level enforcement is not a constitutional seminar. Officers may:

- Misunderstand the law
- Rely on department myths
- Assume compliance equals legality
- Count on citizens not knowing their rights

This does not change the law.
Courts, not officers, define constitutional boundaries.

## The Big Picture for Cop Watchers

Cop watching challenges authority **without breaking the law**. That is why it sometimes provokes resistance.

The Constitution anticipates this tension—and resolves it in favor of the people.

When police attempt to:

- Escalate lawful observation
- Criminalize scrutiny
- Silence critics indirectly

These additional amendments stand as backstops, ensuring that **watching power never becomes a punishable act**.

# Chapter 6 — Case Law That Protects Cop Watchers

Constitutional rights are not enforced by words alone. They are enforced by **court decisions**—case law that interprets the Constitution and binds police departments, officers, and governments.

For cop watchers, case law is critical because it answers the question officers often avoid:

> **"What have courts actually said about recording police?"**

The answer is clear, consistent, and overwhelmingly in favor of the public.

Across the United States, federal courts have repeatedly held that **citizens have a constitutional right to observe and record police performing their duties in public**, subject only to narrow and reasonable limits.

This chapter explains the legal principles—not just the case names—so you understand **why** the law protects you.

## The Core Legal Principle

Federal courts agree on this foundational rule:

> **The First Amendment protects the right to record police officers performing their official duties in public spaces.**

This protection exists because:

- Recording is information gathering
- Information gathering is necessary for speech and press
- Police are government officials acting under public authority

No federal appellate court has ruled that peaceful, non-interfering recording of police in public is illegal.

## Recording Police Is First Amendment–Protected Activity

Multiple federal courts have recognized that:

- Filming police is expressive conduct
- Preventing recording suppresses future speech
- The right belongs to citizens, not just journalists

Courts have explicitly rejected arguments that:

- Only the press may record
- Recording requires permission
- Officers may stop recording based on discomfort

The law does not protect police from embarrassment. It protects the public from unchecked authority.

## Police Have No Reasonable Expectation of Privacy in Public

Courts consistently hold that:

- Police officers performing official duties in public have **no reasonable expectation of privacy**
- Citizens may photograph, film, or record what they can lawfully see or hear

This principle applies to:

- Traffic stops
- Arrests
- Street encounters
- Crowd control
- Protests
- Sidewalk interactions

If an officer can lawfully observe the public, the public can lawfully observe the officer.

## Recording Alone Is Not Interference

One of the most important findings across case law is this:

> **Recording police does not constitute interference, obstruction, or disorderly conduct by itself.**

Courts require **actual obstruction**, such as:

- Physical interference
- Blocking movement
- Preventing lawful commands from being carried out

Mere presence, filming, narration, or criticism **does not meet that standard.**

Officers cannot redefine "interference" to include scrutiny.

## Retaliation for Recording Is Unconstitutional

Courts have repeatedly ruled that police may not:

- Arrest someone for recording
- Detain someone to stop recording
- Threaten arrest to silence filming
- Use pretextual charges to punish observers

If police action is motivated by:

- Dislike of recording
- Anger at criticism
- Desire to stop documentation

That action violates the First Amendment—even if an officer later claims an alternative reason.

Retaliatory arrests are unlawful.

## Fourth Amendment Case Law: Detention Requires Justification

Courts have also been clear that:

- Filming police does not create reasonable suspicion
- Recording does not justify a stop
- Observation does not justify an ID demand

Detentions require:

- Specific facts
- A connection to a real crime
- Articulable reasoning

Stopping someone "to find out what they're doing" because they are filming is not lawful policing.

## Search and Seizure of Cameras and Phones

Case law strongly protects recording devices.

Courts have ruled that:

- Police may not search phones without a warrant
- Police may not delete footage
- Police may not destroy recordings
- Police may not seize devices without legal justification

A phone is not just a camera—it is a container of private data, and the Constitution treats it accordingly.

Even during arrest, digital searches are heavily restricted.

## Qualified Immunity Is Not Absolute

Police sometimes rely on **qualified immunity** to avoid accountability. However:

- Qualified immunity does not protect clearly established rights
- The right to record police has been clearly established

in many jurisdictions for years

As case law has grown more consistent, courts have increasingly rejected immunity defenses where officers interfere with lawful recording.

Ignorance of the law is not a defense for police.

## Circuit Differences (And Why They Still Protect You)

While some federal circuits recognized the right to record earlier than others, courts now broadly agree on the principle.

Even in areas where precedent developed later:

- Police are still bound by constitutional standards
- Retaliation, seizure, and unlawful detention remain illegal
- Departments are expected to train officers accordingly

The trend in case law has moved **one direction only**: toward stronger protection for cop watchers.

## What Case Law Does NOT Require You to Do

Courts have made clear that cop watchers are **not required** to:

- Identify themselves (absent lawful detention and state law)
- Explain why they are recording
- Stop filming because of policy
- Obtain consent from officers

- Remain silent about misconduct

Your obligation is to remain **lawful**, not cooperative.

## Why Case Law Matters on the Street

Police may:

- Misstate the law
- Bluff
- Threaten charges that won't hold up
- Rely on fear or uncertainty

Case law is what courts rely on—not police opinion.

You do not need to argue case names during an encounter. You need only to:

- Remain calm
- Stay non-interfering
- Assert your rights
- Preserve evidence

The law is enforced **after the fact**, not by winning roadside debates.

## The Big Picture

Case law confirms what the Constitution promised:

- Power must tolerate observation
- Accountability requires documentation
- Citizens do not need permission to watch the state

Cop watching is not a loophole.
It is not tolerated behavior.
It is **settled constitutional law**.

# Chapter 7 — What Police Can Lawfully Order (and What They Cannot)

One of the most effective tools police use against cop watchers is **command presence**—issuing orders in a confident tone and relying on the assumption that citizens must comply simply because an officer said so.

The Constitution does not work that way.

Police authority is **limited, conditional, and situation-specific**. Some orders are lawful. Many are not. Knowing the difference is what keeps a lawful act of observation from turning into an unlawful surrender of rights.

This chapter explains **which police orders carry legal force—and which are merely attempts at control**.

## Lawful Orders vs. Unlawful Orders

A police order is lawful only if **all** of the following are true:

1. The officer has legal authority in that situation
2. The order is connected to a legitimate law enforcement purpose
3. The order is reasonable in scope
4. The order does not violate constitutional rights

If any one of these elements is missing, the order is not lawful—even if it is delivered forcefully.

# Orders Police Can Lawfully Give to Cop Watchers

## 1. Lawful Distance or Safety Orders

Police may order you to move back **only when**:

- There is a real, articulable safety concern
- You are physically too close to an active operation
- The distance demanded is reasonable and specific

A lawful distance order:

- Explains the safety issue
- Allows continued observation and recording
- Is not designed to eliminate documentation

An unlawful distance order:

- Is vague ("get back" with no guidance)
- Pushes you out of sight or earshot
- Exists solely to stop filming

You may comply with a lawful distance order **and continue recording.**

## 2. Orders During a Lawful Detention

If you are lawfully detained (based on reasonable suspicion of a crime), police may:

- Order you to stay

- Conduct a limited frisk for weapons if justified
- Ask identifying questions (subject to state law)

Detention must be **temporary and purpose-driven**. It cannot be used to punish observation.

### 3. Orders Related to Crowd Control or Emergencies

During real emergencies or active crime scenes, police may issue orders to:

- Clear an area
- Prevent physical interference
- Maintain public safety

These orders must still be:

- Content-neutral
- Evenly applied
- Limited to the emergency

Police may not use "scene control" as a pretext to suppress recording alone.

## Orders Police Cannot Lawfully Give to Cop Watchers

### 1. "Stop Recording"

Police cannot order you to stop recording simply because:

- They do not consent
- They cite department policy
- They feel uncomfortable
- They claim "you're interfering" without facts

There is **no general power** to prohibit recording in public.

## 2. "Delete That Footage"

Police may never lawfully order you to:

- Delete video
- Delete photos
- Destroy recordings

Deleting footage is destruction of evidence and a serious constitutional violation.

## 3. "Give Me Your Phone" (Without a Warrant)

Police cannot seize or search your phone unless:

- They have a valid warrant, or
- There is a true, immediate exigency

Filming police does not create exigent circumstances.

## 4. "Identify Yourself" (Absent Lawful Detention and State Law)

Police may not demand ID simply because:

- You are filming

- You criticized police
- They want to know who you are

If you are not lawfully detained—and if state law does not require ID during detention—you may lawfully refuse.

### 5. "Explain What You're Doing"

You are never required to:

- Explain your purpose
- Justify your presence
- Answer investigative questions

Silence is constitutional.

### 6. "This Is a Policy"

Police policies:

- Do not override the Constitution
- Do not create new authority
- Do not bind citizens

Only law and constitutional standards matter.

## Commands vs. Requests

Police often blur the line between **requests** and **commands**.

A request:

- Is voluntary

- May be declined
- Does not carry penalties

A command:

- Requires lawful authority
- Must be obeyed if lawful

Officers may phrase requests as commands to test compliance.

A simple clarifying question is powerful:

**"Is that a lawful order?"**

## What Happens If You Disobey an Unlawful Order

Disobeying an unlawful order is **not a crime**—but police may still escalate.

This is why cop watching is about:

- Preserving evidence
- Staying calm
- Avoiding physical resistance

You do not need to "win" the encounter. You need to **survive it legally**.

The Constitution protects you **after the fact**, through courts and accountability mechanisms.

## Why Police Rely on Unlawful Orders

Unlawful orders work because:

- Many people do not know their rights
- Compliance is mistaken for legality
- Officers face little immediate consequence

Cop watchers change that dynamic by being informed, calm, and observant.

## The Golden Rule for Cop Watchers

Remember this:

> **Police may give orders—but only lawful orders must be obeyed.**

Everything else is a request, a bluff, or an attempt to assert control beyond constitutional limits.

Cop watching is not about defiance.

It is about **constitutional discipline**.

# Chapter 8 — What Counts as "Interference" (and What Absolutely Does Not)

Few words are misused by police as often as **"interference."** It is frequently invoked to silence cop watchers, justify unlawful orders, or threaten arrest when officers are uncomfortable with being observed. The Constitution does not allow that.

**Interference has a legal meaning.** Discomfort does not qualify. Criticism does not qualify. Filming does not qualify.

This chapter draws a clear line between **actual interference**, which police may lawfully prevent, and **protected conduct**, which they may not.

## The Legal Meaning of Interference

Interference requires **active, material obstruction** of lawful police duties.

In constitutional terms, interference generally means conduct that:

- Physically blocks officers
- Prevents them from carrying out a lawful action
- Creates an immediate safety risk
- Directly disrupts an arrest, search, or emergency response

Interference is about **what you do**, not **what you record**.

## What Is NOT Interference (Even If Police

## Say It Is)

The following actions are **constitutionally protected** when done lawfully in public:

- Filming or photographing police
- Livestreaming police activity
- Standing nearby at a reasonable distance
- Narrating events
- Taking notes
- Asking lawful questions
- Criticizing police conduct
- Verbally disagreeing with officers
- Remaining silent
- Refusing consent to searches
- Watching without engaging

Police irritation does not transform these actions into crimes.

## Annoyance Is Not Obstruction

Courts have repeatedly rejected the idea that:

- Officer frustration
- Embarrassment
- Nervousness
- Anger at criticism

constitutes interference.

Police are **public officials**. The Constitution assumes they will be observed, criticized, and recorded. Enduring that scrutiny is part of the job.

## Speech Alone Is Almost Never Interference

Verbal speech becomes interference only in rare circumstances, such as:

- True threats
- Commands to others that directly disrupt lawful police action
- Speech that incites immediate violence

Mere commentary—even loud, harsh, or insulting commentary—is protected by the First Amendment.

You may lawfully:

- Call out misconduct
- Question legality
- Tell others their rights
- Criticize police decisions

So long as you are not physically obstructing police or inciting violence, speech remains protected.

## Distance Matters — But Only Reasonably

Distance is relevant **only when tied to safety or operations.**

You may be ordered to move back if:

- You are physically close to an arrest
- You are blocking movement
- You are creating a real safety hazard

However:

- Distance orders must be specific
- They must be reasonable
- They must still allow observation

An order that pushes you out of sight or earshot **solely to stop recording** is not lawful.

Complying with a lawful distance order **does not eliminate your right to record**.

## Recording During Arrests Is Not Interference

Filming an arrest—even a tense or physical one—is lawful if you are not:

- Touching officers or suspects
- Blocking movement
- Refusing lawful safety orders

Police may not declare an arrest "off limits" to the public simply because it involves force.

In fact, arrests are precisely the moments where public oversight matters most.

## Crowds, Protests, and Multiple Observers

The presence of multiple cop watchers does not automatically create interference.

Police must still show:

- Specific disruption
- Actual obstruction
- A legitimate safety concern

They may not:

- Target individual cop watchers
- Apply rules selectively
- Suppress recording while allowing other observation

Equal protection matters.

## Common Police Claims — and the Reality

**"You're interfering."**

→ Ask: *How, specifically?*

**"You're distracting me."**

→ Distraction is not obstruction.

**"You're making this unsafe."**

→ Safety must be articulable, not speculative.

**"This is an active scene."**

→ Active does not mean unobservable.

**"You're escalating the situation."**

→ Recording does not escalate by itself.

## What Actually Counts as Interference

To be clear, interference can occur if you:

- Physically block officers
- Touch police or suspects
- Refuse lawful safety commands
- Enter restricted crime-scene areas
- Incite others to obstruct police

Cop watching is about **observation**, not participation.

## Why Police Stretch the Definition

Police sometimes expand "interference" because:

- Observation challenges authority
- Recording shifts narrative control
- Accountability increases risk of discipline

The Constitution does not permit officers to redefine crimes to avoid scrutiny.

## The Practical Rule for Cop Watchers

If you follow these principles, you are not interfering:

- Keep your hands to yourself
- Maintain reasonable distance
- Do not block movement
- Do not touch evidence
- Do not incite others

- Record openly and calmly

Everything else—tone, criticism, presence—is protected.

## The Bottom Line

Remember this rule:

> **If you are not physically obstructing police or creating a real safety risk, you are not interfering—no matter how uncomfortable officers feel.**

Cop watching is lawful precisely because it is passive, visible, and restrained.

Interference requires action.

Observation requires only presence.

# Chapter 9 — Detention, Arrest, and Retaliation: When Police Cross the Line

Cop watching most often becomes dangerous—not physically, but legally—when police **shift from observation to control**. This shift usually takes one of three forms: detention, arrest, or retaliation. Each is governed by strict constitutional rules. Each is frequently abused when officers are challenged by scrutiny.

This chapter explains **where lawful authority ends and constitutional violations begin**, and how cop watchers can recognize the moment police cross that line.

## Detention: The First Escalation

A detention occurs when a reasonable person would believe they are **not free to leave**.

Detention does **not** require:

- Handcuffs
- Formal arrest language
- Being placed in a car

It **does** occur when:

- You are ordered to stay
- Your movement is blocked
- An officer retains your ID
- You are surrounded or cornered

## Detention Requires Reasonable Suspicion

Police may detain a person **only if** they have reasonable suspicion that the person is involved in a specific crime.

Reasonable suspicion must be:

- Based on articulable facts
- More than a hunch
- Connected to criminal activity

**Cop watching does not qualify.**

If police cannot name a crime you are suspected of committing, the detention is unlawful.

## Detention Cannot Be Used as Intimidation

Police sometimes detain cop watchers to:

- "Check them out"
- Identify critics
- Slow or stop recording
- Assert dominance

Detention for these reasons is unconstitutional.

The Fourth Amendment does not allow detention as a punishment or warning.

# Arrest: The Highest Threshold

An arrest is a **full seizure of liberty** and requires **probable cause**, a higher standard than reasonable suspicion.

Probable cause requires:

- Facts that would lead a reasonable person to believe a crime was committed
- Evidence linking the individual to that crime

Recording police does not create probable cause.

Criticizing police does not create probable cause.

Refusing to answer questions does not create probable cause.

## Pretextual Arrests

A pretextual arrest occurs when police:

- Arrest someone for a minor or fabricated charge
- Use that charge to punish lawful behavior
- Attempt to justify retaliation after the fact

Courts scrutinize these arrests carefully—especially when they follow protected First Amendment activity.

If arrest follows filming, criticism, or refusal to stop recording, **retaliation becomes a central legal issue.**

# Retaliation: A First Amendment Violation

Retaliation occurs when police take adverse action **because of protected activity**.

Protected activity includes:

- Recording police
- Observing police

- Criticizing police
- Refusing consent
- Remaining silent

Retaliatory actions include:

- Detention
- Arrest
- Threats
- Equipment seizure
- Harassment

If the motivating factor behind police action is your exercise of constitutional rights, the action is unlawful—even if an officer later claims a different justification.

### Timing Matters

Courts often look at:

- The sequence of events
- Officer statements
- Escalation immediately after filming begins
- Lack of independent criminal conduct

When police action follows protected conduct closely, retaliation is easier to prove.

## Selective Enforcement and Equal Protection

If police:

- Allow others to observe
- Ignore similar conduct by bystanders
- Target only cop watchers

This raises **Fourteenth Amendment equal protection concerns.**

Law enforcement may not enforce laws selectively based on viewpoint or criticism.

## What to Do During Detention or Arrest

### If Detained

- Ask: "Am I being detained?"
- Ask: "What crime am I suspected of?"
- Invoke your right to remain silent
- Do not consent to searches

### If Arrested

- Stop speaking immediately
- Clearly invoke your right to remain silent
- Ask for a lawyer
- Do not resist physically

You do not win constitutional battles on the street. You preserve them for court.

## Documentation Is Your Best Protection

If possible:

- Keep recording
- Narrate calmly
- State the date, time, and location
- Note badge numbers and names
- Preserve footage immediately

Police may control your body—but they cannot lawfully erase the record.

## Why Retaliation Happens

Retaliation occurs because:

- Cop watching disrupts narrative control
- Video creates accountability
- Observation limits discretion

The Constitution anticipates this friction—and resolves it in favor of the public.

## The Constitutional Red Line

Remember this principle:

> **Police may enforce the law—but they may not punish the exercise of rights.**

The moment police action is motivated by your observation rather than lawful enforcement, **they have crossed a constitutional line.**

Cop watching does not provoke illegality.

It exposes it.

# Chapter 10 — Seizure of Cameras, Phones, and Evidence

For cop watchers, few threats are as serious—or as common—as the attempted seizure of recording devices. Cameras and phones are not just tools; they are **evidence**. When police try to take, search, delete, or destroy recordings, they are often attempting to erase accountability after the fact.

The Constitution places **strict limits** on when—and how—police may interfere with your devices. This chapter explains those limits clearly and practically.

## Your Phone Is Not Just a Camera

Modern courts recognize that a smartphone is fundamentally different from other physical objects. It contains:

- Photos and videos
- Communications
- Location data
- Personal records
- Private thoughts

Because of this, **phones receive heightened constitutional protection**.

Police authority over your phone is far more limited than their authority over ordinary property.

## The General Rule: No Warrant, No Search

As a baseline principle:

> **Police may not search the contents of your phone without a warrant.**

This includes:

- Scrolling through videos
- Reviewing photos
- Watching recordings
- Opening apps
- Accessing cloud storage

This rule applies even if:

- You are detained
- You are arrested
- The phone is locked or unlocked

An arrest does **not** automatically give police the right to search your digital data.

## Police May Not Delete or Order Deletion of Footage

Police may **never** lawfully:

- Order you to delete video
- Delete footage themselves

- Threaten you with arrest to force deletion
- Destroy recordings

Deleting footage is:

- Destruction of evidence
- A violation of the First Amendment
- A violation of the Fourth Amendment
- Often a violation of departmental policy and criminal law

Any officer who orders deletion is acting outside constitutional authority.

## Seizure of Devices: Narrow and Rare

Police may seize a phone or camera **only under limited circumstances**, such as:

- With a valid warrant
- With probable cause that the device itself is evidence of a crime **and**
- When seizure is reasonable in scope

Even then:

- Seizure does not automatically allow searching
- The device must be preserved, not accessed

Filming police does **not** make your device contraband or evidence of a crime.

## The "Exigent Circumstances" Myth

Police sometimes claim they may seize or search a phone due to "exigent circumstances."

Exigency exists only when:

- There is an immediate threat
- Evidence will be destroyed imminently
- No time exists to obtain a warrant

Courts interpret exigency **very narrowly**.

The mere fact that video exists does not create exigency.

The fear that footage might later be shared does not create exigency.

Cloud backups and delayed warrants eliminate most exigency claims.

## Forced Unlocking and Passwords

Police may not lawfully:

- Force you to reveal a password
- Force you to unlock your phone verbally
- Compel you to explain how to access your device

Biometric unlocking (fingerprint or face) is legally contested and varies by jurisdiction, but passwords and passcodes receive strong Fifth Amendment protection.

Best practice:

- Use a passcode

- Disable biometric unlocking when filming police

## Consent Is How Rights Are Lost

Police often ask for consent because:

- Consent bypasses warrant requirements
- Consent is easier than justification
- Many people do not know they can refuse

You may lawfully say:

**"I do not consent to any searches or seizures."**

Refusing consent:

- Is not suspicious
- Is not a crime
- Does not justify escalation

Never volunteer footage on the street.

## What to Do If Police Take Your Device

If police seize your phone or camera:

- Do not resist physically
- State clearly that you do not consent
- Ask if the device is being seized as evidence
- Ask for a receipt or property record
- Remember badge numbers and names

Immediately after release:

- Write down everything you remember
- Preserve backups
- Contact a lawyer

The legality of the seizure is decided later—not on the scene.

## Preserving Evidence as a Cop Watcher

Best practices include:

- Use cloud backups or livestreaming
- Lock your phone quickly
- Narrate what is happening
- State the date, time, and location
- Avoid touching your phone unnecessarily once seized

Evidence that survives is evidence that holds power accountable.

## Why Police Target Devices

Police target cameras and phones because:

- Video limits narrative control
- Evidence contradicts reports
- Accountability follows documentation

The Constitution does not allow officers to solve this problem by silencing the public.

## The Core Rule for Cop Watchers

Remember this principle:

> **Police may control scenes—but they may not control the record.**

Your recordings are protected because democracy requires proof, not permission.

Cop watching does not end when recording stops.

It ends when accountability begins.

# Chapter 11 — Cop Watching in Practice: Best Practices, Scripts, and Survival

Knowing the law is essential—but **how you apply it in real life** is what determines whether cop watching remains safe, effective, and legally protected. Most constitutional violations do not happen because a cop watcher is wrong; they happen because police exploit confusion, fear, or escalation.

This chapter translates everything you've learned so far into **practical, street-level guidance** designed to keep you lawful, calm, and protected—before, during, and after encounters.

## The Cop Watcher Mindset

Cop watching is not about confrontation. It is about **presence, restraint, and documentation**.

A calm cop watcher:

- Does not argue emotionally
- Does not escalate verbally
- Does not chase authority
- Does not try to "win" the encounter

Your goal is not compliance—but **preservation**:

- Preserve your rights
- Preserve your freedom
- Preserve the record

The Constitution works best when paired with discipline.

## Before You Start Recording

### Choose Your Position

- Stay in public spaces
- Avoid blocking sidewalks or streets
- Maintain a reasonable distance
- Keep an escape route if possible

### Prepare Your Device

- Enable screen lock
- Use a strong passcode
- Disable biometric unlock if possible
- Enable cloud backup or livestreaming

### Know Your Role

You are an observer, not a participant.

You are a witness, not an enforcer.

You are documenting the state—not directing it.

## While Recording Police

### Best Practices

- Hold your camera steady
- Record continuously when possible
- Narrate calmly and factually
- State date, time, and location
- Avoid profanity if possible (it's protected—but

clarity matters)

### Do Not

- Touch officers or suspects
- Physically intervene
- Block movement
- Yell commands
- Crowd officers unnecessarily

Visibility protects you. Chaos does not.

## What to Say (and What Not to Say)

### Safe, Effective Phrases

- "I am recording."
- "I'm exercising my First Amendment rights."
- "Am I being detained, or am I free to go?"
- "I do not consent to any searches."
- "I choose to remain silent."

Say these calmly and clearly—once if possible.

### What Not to Say

Avoid:

- Explaining your intentions
- Debating the law
- Answering investigative questions

- Making jokes or sarcastic remarks
- Threatening lawsuits on the scene

Anything you say can be misunderstood or misquoted.

## If Police Approach You

Police may:

- Ask questions
- Request cooperation
- Attempt to control the interaction

You may:

- Remain silent
- Continue recording
- Walk away if not detained
- Decline consent

Ask the key question early:

**"Am I being detained?"**

This clarifies the legal posture of the encounter.

## If Police Order You to Move

Ask yourself:

- Is this order specific?
- Is it tied to safety?

- Does it still allow observation?

If yes, comply and continue recording.

If no, you may still choose to comply for safety—but **note the order on camera**.

Compliance does not equal legality.

Documentation preserves the issue for later.

## If Police Threaten Arrest

Threats are often used to:

- Intimidate
- Test compliance
- Stop recording

Stay calm.

Do not argue.

Do not escalate.

Say:

"I am exercising my rights."

Then say nothing more.

## If You Are Detained

- Stop engaging
- Invoke your right to remain silent
- Do not consent to searches
- Continue recording if possible

- Do not physically resist

Detention must be justified. Your job is not to justify yourself—it is to **preserve evidence.**

## If You Are Arrested

Arrest is not the end of your rights—it is the point where new protections begin.

### Immediately

- Stop speaking
- Say: "I am exercising my right to remain silent."
- Say: "I want a lawyer."

Do not explain.
Do not negotiate.
Do not answer "just a few questions."

## After the Encounter

As soon as possible:

- Write down everything you remember
- Preserve footage and backups
- Note badge numbers, names, vehicles
- Record time, date, and location
- Contact a lawyer or civil rights organization if necessary

Memory fades. Records matter.

## Why Calm Wins

Police encounters are often chaotic by design. Calm behavior:

- De-escalates risk
- Strengthens your legal position
- Improves credibility
- Preserves constitutional claims

Judges do not evaluate rights in a vacuum—they evaluate **conduct, context, and credibility**.

A calm cop watcher is a powerful one.

## Cop Watching Is a Long Game

Cop watching is not about a single video or encounter. It is about:

- Normalizing accountability
- Building public records
- Creating institutional pressure
- Reinforcing constitutional culture

Every lawful recording strengthens precedent.

Every calm witness reinforces the rule of law.

## The Final Practical Rule

Remember this:

**You do not need to convince police you are right—you only need to remain lawful.**

The Constitution does not require you to be loud.
It requires you to be **present**.

# Chapter 12 — Cop Watcher Pocket Guide, Rights Summary, and Final Notes

Cop watching is not about knowing *everything*. It is about knowing **enough**—enough to remain lawful, enough to preserve evidence, and enough to prevent intimidation from becoming compliance.

This final chapter distills the Constitution into a **usable field guide**, followed by closing principles that explain *why* cop watching matters in a free society.

## The Cop Watcher Pocket Guide

### Your Core Constitutional Rights

**You have the right to:**

- Observe police in public
- Record police performing official duties
- Stand at a reasonable distance
- Criticize police verbally
- Remain silent
- Refuse consent to searches
- Walk away if not detained
- Ask if you are being detained
- Ask for a lawyer if arrested

**You do NOT have to:**

- Explain why you are filming

- Identify yourself unless lawfully detained and state law requires it
- Stop recording because of "policy"
- Delete footage
- Unlock your phone
- Answer questions
- Consent to searches

## Am I Being Detained? — The One Question That Matters

Ask clearly:

**"Am I being detained, or am I free to go?"**

- If **free to go** → leave or continue recording
- If **detained** → remain silent and do not consent to searches

This question forces officers to choose legality over ambiguity.

## What to Say — Minimal, Effective Language

Use calm, short statements:

- "I am recording."
- "I'm exercising my rights."
- "I do not consent to any searches."
- "I am exercising my right to remain silent."

- "I want a lawyer."

Say it once if possible. Then stop talking.

## What to Avoid Saying

Avoid:

- Explaining your purpose
- Debating the law
- Justifying your presence
- Answering investigative questions
- Threatening lawsuits on the scene

Street encounters are not courtrooms.

## Distance and Interference Checklist

You are **not interfering** if you:

- Are in a public place
- Maintain reasonable distance
- Do not block officers
- Do not touch anyone
- Do not incite others
- Comply with lawful safety orders

Observation ≠ obstruction.

## Device Protection Checklist

Before filming:

- Use a passcode
- Disable biometric unlock if possible
- Enable cloud backup or livestreaming

If police demand your phone:

- State you do not consent
- Do not resist physically
- Do not unlock the device
- Remember badge numbers and names

Police may not lawfully delete or destroy footage.

## If Things Go Wrong

### If Detained

- Remain silent
- Do not consent to searches
- Continue recording if possible

### If Arrested

- Stop speaking
- Invoke your right to remain silent
- Ask for a lawyer
- Do not resist physically

Preserve your case for later.

## The Constitutional Logic of Cop

## Watching

Cop watching exists because the Constitution assumes three things:

1. **Power must be limited**
2. **Power resists oversight**
3. **Liberty depends on witnesses**

The Framers did not trust authority to police itself. That is why:

- Speech is protected
- Silence is protected
- Privacy is protected
- Accountability is baked into the system

Cop watching is not hostile to law enforcement.
It is faithful to constitutional design.

## Why Cop Watching Matters

Cop watching:

- Preserves evidence
- Protects the innocent
- Deters abuse
- Strengthens public trust
- Reinforces constitutional culture

When misconduct is documented, it can be challenged.

When conduct is visible, it improves.

Transparency protects everyone—including good officers.

## Final Rule to Remember

If you remember nothing else from this book, remember this:

> **Police authority ends where constitutional rights begin.**

You do not need permission to watch power.

You do not need approval to document it.

You do not need to explain yourself to exercise your rights.

You only need to remain lawful.

## Conclusion — Watching the Watchers Is a Civic Duty

Cop watching is not radical.

It is not dangerous.

It is not anti-police.

It is **constitutional citizenship**.

A free society does not rely on silence.

It relies on witnesses.

And in the United States, the Constitution guarantees the right to be one.

## All the Features of the First Amendment — Media & Press Protections

The **First Amendment** protects far more than newspapers and television stations. Its media protections apply to **any person engaged in gathering, recording, creating, or distributing information** about government activity. In constitutional law, "media" describes **function**, not status.

Below is a complete, structured breakdown of **every major First Amendment feature as it applies to media, recording, and cop watching.**

## 1. Freedom of the Press (Core Media Protection)

The Press Clause states that government may not abridge the freedom of the press.

**What this actually means:**

- The government cannot control who may gather information
- The government cannot license journalism
- The government cannot punish publication of lawful material
- The government cannot suppress documentation of public officials

**Key point:**
You do **not** need to be a journalist.

If you are recording, documenting, photographing, or publishing—you are exercising press freedom.

## 2. Information Gathering Is Protected

Courts recognize that **press freedom is meaningless without the right to gather information**.

Protected media activities include:

- Filming police
- Photographing government officials
- Audio recording in public
- Livestreaming public events
- Taking notes
- Documenting arrests and traffic stops
- Observing public officials at work

Stopping recording is legally treated as **preventing future speech**.

## 3. No Licensing, Credentials, or Permission

The First Amendment forbids:

- Press licensing schemes
- Mandatory credentials to record
- Permission requirements to document public officials
- Government approval of who counts as "media"

A citizen with a phone has the **same constitutional protection** as a news organization.

## 4. Content Neutrality

Government restrictions on media must be **content-neutral.**

This means police **cannot**:

- Stop recording because it is critical
- Allow favorable filming but block critical filming
- Target cop watchers while allowing tourists or reporters

Viewpoint discrimination is unconstitutional.

## 5. Protection Against Prior Restraint

**Prior restraint** is government action that stops speech *before* it happens.

The First Amendment strongly prohibits:

- Ordering recording to stop
- Seizing cameras to prevent publication
- Threatening arrest to silence documentation
- Deleting footage

Prior restraint is one of the **most serious First Amendment violations.**

## 6. Publication Is Protected (Even If Embarrassing)

Once information is lawfully obtained:

- The government may not punish its publication
- Embarrassment to officials is irrelevant
- Truthful reporting about public officials is protected

This applies to:

- Social media
- YouTube
- Livestreams
- Blogs
- Independent platforms

## 7. Anonymous Media Is Protected

The First Amendment protects:

- Anonymous speech
- Anonymous publication
- Anonymous recording
- Anonymous distribution of media

You do **not** have to identify yourself to record or publish.

## 8. No Duty to Be Neutral or "Objective"

The First Amendment does **not** require:

- Neutral tone
- Balanced commentary
- Respectful language
- Objectivity

Media may be:

- Critical
- Opinionated
- Harsh
- One-sided

Cop watching does not lose protection because it is critical of police.

## 9. Protection for New Technology

First Amendment media protections apply to:

- Smartphones
- Body cams
- Dash cams
- Drones (with airspace limits)
- Livestreaming platforms
- Social media

The Constitution protects **activities**, not technologies.

## 10. Time, Place, and Manner Limits (Narrow Exception)

Media activity may be limited **only if** restrictions are:

1. Content-neutral
2. Narrowly tailored to a real government interest
3. Leave open alternative ways to record

Police **may not** use this doctrine to eliminate recording entirely.

## 11. Protection Against Retaliation

Government officials may not retaliate against media activity.

Retaliation includes:

- Detention for filming
- Arrest for recording
- Equipment seizure to punish documentation
- Harassment meant to chill recording

Retaliation violates the First Amendment even if police later claim a pretext.

## 12. Equal Access to Public Space

Media may operate anywhere the public is lawfully allowed to be.

Police may not:

- Create media-free zones

- Exclude citizen journalists
- Restrict recording only for critics

Public space = public documentation rights.

## 13. Recording Audio and Video

In public:

- Video recording is protected
- Audio recording of police performing official duties is protected
- Officers have no privacy expectation while working publicly

Wiretap laws **cannot** be used to criminalize cop watching.

## 14. No Seizure or Destruction of Media

The First Amendment prohibits:

- Deleting recordings
- Destroying cameras
- Seizing devices without warrants
- Ordering deletion

Media materials receive **heightened constitutional protection**.

## 15. Media Is a Check on Government Power

At its core, the First Amendment treats media as:

- A watchdog
- A check on authority
- A safeguard against abuse
- A pillar of democratic accountability

Cop watching is a **modern expression of this role.**

## One-Sentence Summary

**The First Amendment protects every person's right to gather, record, publish, and criticize information about government officials—without permission, credentials, or fear of retaliation.**

# Appendix A — Case-Law That Protects Cop Watchers (Named Rulings)

This appendix lists **key U.S. court decisions by name**, with plain-language explanations of what each case established. Together, these rulings form the modern legal backbone protecting the right to observe, record, and criticize police in public.

You do **not** need to memorize these cases or cite them on the street. They exist so that **courts, lawyers, and judges** can hold police accountable *after* an encounter.

# I. First Amendment — The Right to Record Police

## Glik v. Cunniffe (1st Cir. 2011)

**Holding:** Citizens have a First Amendment right to record police officers performing their duties in public.

**Why it matters:**

This is one of the most influential cop-watching cases in U.S. history. The court explicitly stated that:

- Recording police is protected speech
- The right applies to ordinary citizens, not just journalists
- Police have no reasonable expectation of privacy in public

This case is frequently cited nationwide.

## Fields v. City of Philadelphia (3rd Cir. 2017)

**Holding:** The First Amendment protects the act of photographing and recording police in public.

**Why it matters:**

The court rejected the argument that recording must be tied to an explicit expressive purpose. **The act of recording itself is protected.**

## Turner v. Driver (5th Cir. 2017)

**Holding:** The First Amendment protects the right to record police, subject to reasonable time, place, and manner restrictions.

**Why it matters:**

This case confirmed the right in a large portion of the southern U.S. and rejected police claims that filming alone justifies detention.

## ACLU of Illinois v. Alvarez (7th Cir. 2012)

**Holding:** Audio recording of police performing official duties in public is protected by the First Amendment.

**Why it matters:**

The court struck down the use of wiretapping laws against cop watchers and emphasized that **information gathering is a necessary precursor to speech**.

## Smith v. City of Cumming (11th Cir. 2000)

**Holding:** Citizens have a First Amendment right to record police activities, subject to reasonable restrictions.

**Why it matters:**

One of the earliest federal appellate cases recognizing the right to record police.

## II. Retaliation for Recording Police

### Nieves v. Bartlett (U.S. Supreme Court, 2019)

**Holding:** Retaliatory arrest claims are generally barred when probable cause exists—but **not** when officers typically do not arrest for the alleged offense.

**Why it matters:**

The Court left a critical opening for cop watchers:

If police normally ignore a minor offense but suddenly enforce it **because of protected speech**, retaliation claims may proceed.

### Lozman v. City of Riviera Beach (U.S. Supreme Court, 2018)

**Holding:** Retaliatory arrest claims may proceed when retaliation is the motivating factor, even if probable cause exists.

**Why it matters:**

This case protects critics of government officials from being silenced through pretextual arrests.

# III. Fourth Amendment — Detention, Searches, and Seizures

## Terry v. Ohio (U.S. Supreme Court, 1968)

**Holding:** Police may briefly detain a person only with reasonable suspicion of criminal activity.

**Why it matters:**

Cop watching does **not** create reasonable suspicion. Terry sets the baseline that police must justify detentions with specific facts.

## Brown v. Texas (U.S. Supreme Court, 1979)

**Holding:** Police may not stop and demand identification without reasonable suspicion.

**Why it matters:**

This case directly undermines police attempts to demand ID from cop watchers absent lawful detention.

## Hiibel v. Sixth Judicial District Court (U.S. Supreme Court, 2004)

**Holding:** States may require ID **only during a lawful detention** and **only if state law explicitly authorizes it.**

**Why it matters:**

Police often misquote this case. It does **not** authorize random ID demands.

# IV. Phones, Cameras, and Digital Evidence

## Riley v. California (U.S. Supreme Court, 2014)

**Holding:** Police generally may not search a phone without a warrant, even after arrest.

**Why it matters:**

This is the strongest phone-privacy ruling in U.S. law. It applies directly to cop watchers' recordings.

## United States v. Jones (U.S. Supreme Court, 2012)

**Holding:** Long-term electronic surveillance constitutes a search under the Fourth Amendment.

**Why it matters:**

Reinforces that digital data receives heightened constitutional protection.

## Arizona v. Gant (U.S. Supreme Court, 2009)

**Holding:** Searches incident to arrest are limited and do not automatically extend to all personal property.

**Why it matters:**

Police cannot use arrest as a blanket excuse to search devices.

# V. Destruction or Seizure of Recordings

## Roaden v. Kentucky (U.S. Supreme Court, 1973)

**Holding:** Seizing expressive material without a warrant raises serious First Amendment concerns.

**Why it matters:**

Recordings are expressive material. Seizure requires strict justification.

## Stanley v. Georgia (U.S. Supreme Court, 1969)

**Holding:** The state cannot criminalize mere possession of protected expressive material.

**Why it matters:**

Reinforces limits on government control over recorded content.

# VI. Speech, Criticism, and "Disorderly Conduct"

## City of Houston v. Hill (U.S. Supreme Court, 1987)

**Holding:** Laws criminalizing verbal criticism of police are unconstitutional.

**Why it matters:**

Police may not arrest people simply for talking back, criticizing, or challenging authority.

## Norwell v. City of Cincinnati (U.S. Supreme Court, 1973)

**Holding:** Verbal objections to police action are protected speech.

**Why it matters:**

Criticism—even angry criticism—is not interference.

# VII. Qualified Immunity Limits

## Hope v. Pelzer (U.S. Supreme Court, 2002)

**Holding:** Qualified immunity does not protect officers who violate clearly established rights.

**Why it matters:**

As the right to record police becomes well established, immunity defenses weaken.

## VIII. What This Case Law Establishes — In Plain Terms

Together, these rulings confirm that:

- Recording police in public is protected by the First Amendment
- Police may not detain you just for filming
- Police may not demand ID without lawful detention and state authority
- Police may not seize or search your phone without a warrant
- Police may not delete footage
- Police may not retaliate against protected speech
- Criticism of police is not a crime
- "Interference" requires real obstruction, not observation

### Final Legal Reality

No federal court has ruled that peaceful, non-interfering cop watching in public is illegal.

Courts have ruled—again and again—that **the Constitution protects witnesses to power**.

# Appendix A — Citation-Ready Legal Appendix (U.S. Cop-Watching Case Law)

# I. First Amendment — Right to Record Police

Glik v. Cunniffe, 655 F.3d 78 (1st Cir. 2011).

*(Holding that the First Amendment protects the right of a private citizen to record police officers carrying out their duties in public; rejecting claims of officer privacy and qualified immunity.)*

Fields v. City of Philadelphia, 862 F.3d 353 (3d Cir. 2017).

*(Recognizing a First Amendment right to photograph and record police activity in public without needing an expressive purpose beyond recording itself.)*

Turner v. Driver, 848 F.3d 678 (5th Cir. 2017).

*(Holding that the First Amendment protects the right to record police in public, subject only to reasonable time, place, and manner restrictions.)*

ACLU of Illinois v. Alvarez, 679 F.3d 583 (7th Cir. 2012).

*(Striking down application of state wiretapping law to recording police; holding that audio recording police in public is protected First Amendment activity.)*

Smith v. City of Cumming, 212 F.3d 1332 (11th Cir. 2000).

*(Recognizing a First Amendment right to photograph and videotape police conduct, subject to reasonable restrictions.)*

# II. Retaliatory Arrest and Retaliation for Protected Speech

Nieves v. Bartlett, 587 U.S. ___, 139 S. Ct. 1715 (2019).

*(Holding that probable cause generally bars retaliatory arrest claims, but creating an exception where officers typically decline to arrest for the offense and enforcement is motivated by protected speech.)*

Lozman v. City of Riviera Beach, 585 U.S. ___, 138 S. Ct. 1945 (2018).

*(Holding that retaliatory arrest claims may proceed where retaliation is the motivating factor, even if probable cause exists.)*

# III. Fourth Amendment — Detention and Identification

Terry v. Ohio, 392 U.S. 1 (1968).

*(Establishing that police may briefly detain individuals only with reasonable suspicion supported by articulable facts.)*

Brown v. Texas, 443 U.S. 47 (1979).

*(Holding that police may not stop and demand identification without reasonable suspicion of criminal activity.)*

Hiibel v. Sixth Judicial District Court of Nevada, 542 U.S. 177 (2004).

*(Holding that states may require identification only during a lawful Terry stop and only where state law explicitly authorizes such a requirement.)*

# IV. Fourth Amendment — Phones, Cameras, and Digital Evidence

Riley v. California, 573 U.S. 373 (2014).

*(Holding that police generally must obtain a warrant before searching the digital contents of a cell phone, even incident to arrest.)*

United States v. Jones, 565 U.S. 400 (2012).

*(Holding that long-term electronic tracking constitutes a Fourth Amendment search.)*

Arizona v. Gant, 556 U.S. 332 (2009).

*(Limiting the scope of searches incident to arrest and rejecting automatic searches of personal property.)*

# V. Seizure or Destruction of Expressive Material

Roaden v. Kentucky, 413 U.S. 496 (1973).

*(Holding that seizure of expressive materials without a warrant raises serious First Amendment concerns.)*

Stanley v. Georgia, 394 U.S. 557 (1969).

*(Holding that the government may not criminalize mere possession of protected expressive material.)*

# VI. Speech, Criticism, and Disorderly Conduct

City of Houston v. Hill, 482 U.S. 451 (1987).

*(Holding that laws criminalizing verbal criticism or challenge of police officers are unconstitutional.)*

Norwell v. City of Cincinnati, 414 U.S. 14 (1973).

*(Holding that verbal objections to police action are protected speech under the First Amendment.)*

# VII. Qualified Immunity Limits

**Hope v. Pelzer, 536 U.S. 730 (2002).**

***(Holding that qualified immunity does not protect officials who violate clearly established constitutional rights.)***

# VIII. Legal Principles Established by This Case Law

Collectively, these cases establish that:

- Recording police in public is protected First Amendment activity
- Police may not detain individuals solely for filming
- Police may not demand identification absent lawful detention and statutory authority
- Police may not search or seize phones without a warrant or exigent circumstances
- Police may not delete or destroy recordings
- Retaliatory enforcement for protected speech violates the Constitution
- Verbal criticism of police is protected speech
- "Interference" requires actual obstruction, not observation
- Qualified immunity does not shield violations of clearly established rights

## Publication Note / Disclaimer (Optional)

*This appendix is provided for educational and informational purposes only and does not constitute legal advice. Laws and interpretations may vary by jurisdiction. Readers are encouraged to consult a licensed attorney for case-specific guidance.*

# List of References Used in This Book

The following sources informed the constitutional analysis, legal principles, and practical guidance presented throughout this book. References include U.S. Supreme Court decisions, federal appellate rulings, constitutional texts, and authoritative legal materials commonly relied upon in civil-rights litigation and academic analysis.


## Foundational Legal Texts

- The Constitution of the United States of America (Including the Bill of Rights and the Fourteenth Amendment)
- The Federalist Papers (selected essays on limited government, accountability, and civil liberty)

## United States Supreme Court Cases

- *Terry v. Ohio*, 392 U.S. 1 (1968)
- *Brown v. Texas*, 443 U.S. 47 (1979)
- *Hiibel v. Sixth Judicial District Court of Nevada*, 542 U.S. 177 (2004)
- *City of Houston v. Hill*, 482 U.S. 451 (1987)
- *Norwell v. City of Cincinnati*, 414 U.S. 14 (1973)
- *Riley v. California*, 573 U.S. 373 (2014)
- *United States v. Jones*, 565 U.S. 400 (2012)
- *Arizona v. Gant*, 556 U.S. 332 (2009)
- *Stanley v. Georgia*, 394 U.S. 557 (1969)
- *Roaden v. Kentucky*, 413 U.S. 496 (1973)

- *Hope v. Pelzer*, 536 U.S. 730 (2002)
- *Lozman v. City of Riviera Beach*, 138 S. Ct. 1945 (2018)
- *Nieves v. Bartlett*, 139 S. Ct. 1715 (2019)


## United States Federal Appellate Court Cases


- *Glik v. Cunniffe*, 655 F.3d 78 (1st Cir. 2011)
- *Fields v. City of Philadelphia*, 862 F.3d 353 (3d Cir. 2017)
- *Turner v. Driver*, 848 F.3d 678 (5th Cir. 2017)
- *ACLU of Illinois v. Alvarez*, 679 F.3d 583 (7th Cir. 2012)
- *Smith v. City of Cumming*, 212 F.3d 1332 (11th Cir. 2000)


## Constitutional and Civil Rights Scholarship


- Chemerinsky, Erwin. *Constitutional Law: Principles and Policies*.
- Amar, Akhil Reed. *America's Constitution: A Biography*.
- Tribe, Laurence H. *American Constitutional Law*.
- Hall, Ely, Wiecek & Woloch. *The Oxford Companion to the Supreme Court of the United States*.


## Civil Liberties and Legal Advocacy Resources


- American Civil Liberties Union (ACLU), *Know Your Rights* publications

- National Lawyers Guild, *Police Accountability and Observer Rights Materials*
- Electronic Frontier Foundation (EFF), *Recording Law Enforcement and Digital Privacy Guides*

## Additional Legal References

- United States Department of Justice, Civil Rights Division guidance on police conduct
- State and federal criminal procedure treatises addressing search, seizure, and detention
- Federal Judicial Center publications on constitutional litigation

## Author's Note

This book relies on settled constitutional doctrine and widely cited precedent. While specific applications may vary by jurisdiction, the legal principles discussed herein reflect mainstream federal constitutional law as recognized by U.S. courts.

This reference list is intended for educational and informational purposes and does not constitute legal advice.

Did you love *Watching the Watchers*? Then you should read *Watching the Watchers*[1] by Special Ed!

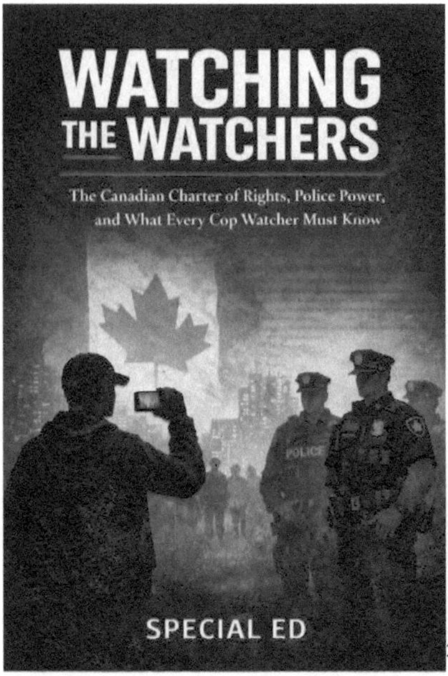

[2]

**WATCHING THE WATCHERS** is a practical, plain-language guide to understanding and asserting your rights under the **Canadian Charter of Rights and Freedoms** during police encounters.

Written for cop watchers, journalists, activists, and everyday Canadians, this book explains what police can—and cannot—lawfully do, when you must show ID (and when you don't), how detention really works, and why recording police in public is protected expression. Drawing on real Charter

1. https://books2read.com/u/meQxKz

2. https://books2read.com/u/meQxKz

principles and Supreme Court rulings, it cuts through myths, intimidation, and misinformation.

This is not anti-police.It is pro-constitution.

If you've ever wondered where your rights begin, where police power ends, and how to protect yourself calmly and lawfully in real time, this book is your field guide.

www.ingramcontent.com/pod-product-compliance
Lightning Source LLC
LaVergne TN
LVHW101616210926
848480LV00009B/604
* 9 7 9 8 2 2 4 9 2 2 0 1 7 *